LIGHTNING
BOLT
BOOKS ™

Magic Disappearing Acts

Elsie Olson

Lerner Publications • Minneapolis

Lerner Publications Company
A division of Lerner Publishing Group, Inc.
241 First Avenue North
Minneapolis, MN 55401 USA

For reading levels and more information, look up this title at www.lernerbooks.com.

Library of Congress Cataloging-in-Publication Data

Names: Olson, Elsie, 1986- author.
Title: Magic disappearing acts / by Elsie Olson.
Other titles: Disappearing acts
Description: Minneapolis, Minnesota : Lerner Publications Company, [2019] | Series: Lightning Bolt Books — Magic tricks | Includes bibliographical references and index. | Audience: Ages: 6-9. | Audience: Grades: K to Grade 3.
Identifiers: LCCN 2018011218 (print) | LCCN 2018018832 (ebook) | ISBN 9781541543379 (eb pdf) | ISBN 9781541538979 (library binding : alk. paper)
Subjects: LCSH: Magic tricks—Juvenile literature. | Magic tricks—Handbooks, manuals, etc.
Classification: LCC GV1555 (ebook) | LCC GV1555 .O57 2019 (print) | DDC 793.8—dc23

LC record available at https://lccn.loc.gov/2018011218

Manufactured in the United States of America
1-45080-35907-7/9/2018

Table of Contents

Getting Started

Have you ever watched a magician perform? There is a secret behind every trick. Magicians perform tricks that make things seem to disappear. With practice, you can do disappearing tricks too!

Disappearing Trick Tips

- **Get permission.** Ask an adult if it's OK to perform these tricks. Make sure you are allowed to use any materials needed. Ask for help when using scissors.

- **Use misdirection.** Is there something you don't want your audience to see? Direct their attention away from it. If you are using your left hand to hide an object, draw attention to your right hand. You can do this by making gestures with your right hand.

- **Practice!** It can take a long time to perfect a trick. Practice in front of a mirror until you are ready.

- **Make each trick your own!** Add a magic word, tell a story, or find another way to make the trick unique.

Not So Tricky

The Vanishing Penny

Mystify your audience when a coin disappears before their very eyes!

What you need:

- Coin

- Table and chair

Getting ready:

Practice holding the coin between your thumb and your pointer and middle fingers. Pay attention to the position of your hand. This is the magic position!

The trick:

1. Sit in the chair with it pulled up close to the edge of the table. Place the coin on the table in front of you. Place one hand in your lap.

2. Place the palm of your other hand over the coin on the table. Sweep the coin toward your body. When you reach the edge

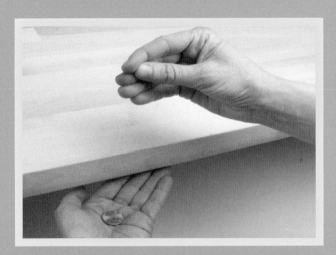

of the table, let the coin drop into the hand in your lap. But put your other hand in the magic position, as if you were still holding the coin.

3. Snap your fingers on your hand that appears to have the coin. Then open your hand to reveal the coin has disappeared!

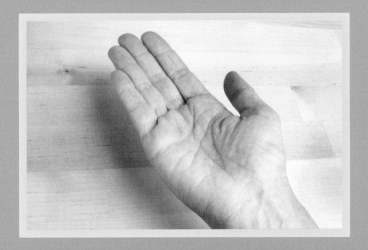

Marvelous Missing Marble

Your audience will wonder where in the world your mysterious marble went!

What you need:

- Paper cup
- Marble
- Scissors

Getting ready:

Carefully cut a hole in the bottom of the cup.

The hole should be large enough for the marble to fit through.

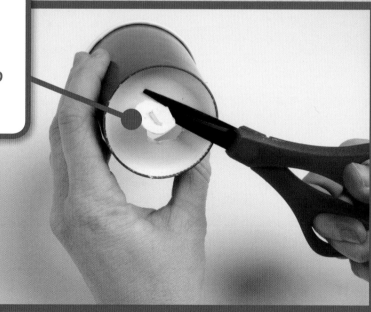

The trick:

1. Show the audience the paper cup. Make sure to hold your hand around the front edge and bottom of the cup so the audience can't see the hole.

2. Explain that this is a very special cup with the power to make things disappear!

3. Drop the marble into the cup. It will fall through the hole and into your cupped hand.

4. Wave your hand over the cup, and say a magic word, like "Abracadabra!" Then take the cup with your free hand and turn the cup upside down. Hold the cup so the audience can't see the hole. At the same time, keep the marble hidden in your other hand. Everyone will think you've made the marble disappear!

A Little Tricky

Where Did the Water Go?

Delight the crowd when you magically turn water into air!

What you need:

- Sponge
- Scissors
- Liquid measuring cup
- Colored cup that you cannot see through
- Water

Getting ready:

1. Carefully cut the sponge into a square that fits tightly into the bottom of the cup. The dry sponge should stay in the cup even when you flip it upside down.

2. Pour a little water into the cup to soak the sponge. Then turn the cup upside down over a sink. If water drains out, you've added too much. Squeeze the water out of the sponge.

3. Repeat step 2 until you find out how much water you can add to the sponge without it leaking out of the cup. This is your magic amount!

4. Fill the measuring cup with this amount of water.

The trick:

1. Show everyone the cup. Don't let them see inside!

2. Pour the water into the cup.

3. Wave your hand over the cup. Say a little rhyme while you do so, like, "Water, water, disappear, air is all I want in here!"
Saying the rhyme gives the sponge a few seconds to soak up the water.

4. Flip the cup upside down. It will seem as if the water has vanished!

Disappear on a Dime

Amaze your friends and family with a magical disappearing dime!

What you need:

- Dime

Getting ready:

Practice this trick in front of a mirror many times before performing it. You want to make your movements smooth and believable.

The trick:

1. Hold your right hand out with the palm up.

Place the dime on the joint where your palm meets your middle finger.

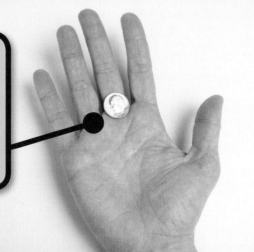

2. Flip your right hand over and pretend to toss the coin into your left hand. As you turn your right hand, slide your right thumb up so it holds the coin in place.

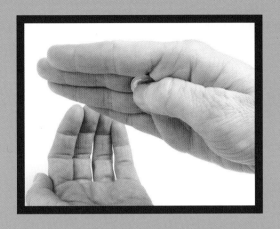

3. Close your left hand as if it were holding the coin. Drop your right hand down to your side. Keep your fingers slightly apart. Your middle finger will hide the coin.

Practice making your right hand look natural while it hides the coin.

4. Bring your closed left hand up to your mouth and blow on it. As you do, open your hand. The audience will think you made the coin disappear!

Now You See It, Now You Don't!

A mysterious towel makes a button vanish.

What you need:

- Clear plastic cup

- 2 sheets of paper, the same color

- Pencil

- Scissors

- All-purpose glue

- Flat object, such as a button

- Dish towel

- Table

Getting ready:

1. Set the cup upside down on a sheet of paper. Trace around the cup's rim with the pencil.

2. Carefully cut out the circle. Put small dots of glue around the circle's edge. Glue the circle to the rim of the cup. Let the glue dry.

3. Place the uncut sheet of paper on the table. Place the button on the paper. Set the cup upside down next to the button.

The trick:

1. Tell the audience you will make the button vanish with your magic towel. *Direct the audience's attention to the towel instead of the cup.*

2. Place the towel over the cup. Then put the towel-covered cup over the button. Knock on the cup and remove the towel. It will look as if the button has vanished!

3. Cover the cup with the towel and knock on the cup again. This time, remove both the towel and cup. It will look as if the button has reappeared!

Terrifically Tricky

Disappearing Hanky

Hide a hanky with this clever trick!

What you need:

- Handkerchief

- Thumb tip
  You can find this prop at most magic stores or online.

Getting ready:

Place the thumb tip over one of your thumbs.

The trick:

1. Hold the handkerchief in the thumb tip hand. Show your audience it is an ordinary hanky. Make sure the hanky is covering the thumb tip.

2. Make a loose fist with the other hand. Use your thumb tip to push a corner of the hanky into the fist. As you do so, grab the thumb tip with your loose fist and pull your real thumb out. Don't let your audience see any part of the thumb tip.

3. Use the fingers of your free hand to push the hanky into the thumb tip. It will look as if you are stuffing the hanky into your fist. Once the hanky is all the way in, slip the thumb tip back onto your thumb. *Once the thumb tip is on, pretend to keep stuffing the hanky into your fist a few more times.*

4. Open your fist. Brush your other hand over your open hand to show that the hanky has vanished!

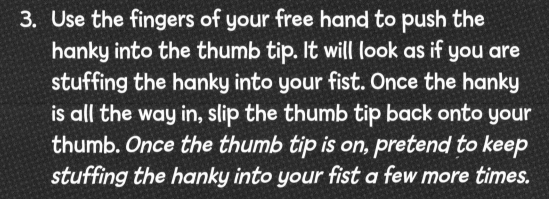

Use the rest of the thumb tip hand to hide the thumb tip from the audience.

Where Did the Cup Go?

Surprise your audience when you seem to accidentally make a cup disappear!

What you need:

- Sheet of paper
- Scissors
- Paper or plastic cup
- Figurine or another small object
- Table and chair

Getting ready:

1. Carefully cut the paper into a large square.

2. Set the cup upside down onto the table. Place the paper square on top of the upside-down cup.

3. Gently squeeze the paper around the cup so the edges of the square reach the table. Make sure you cannot see the cup underneath the paper.

The trick:

1. Sit down, and place the figurine, cup, and paper onto the table. Tell your audience you will make this figurine disappear using the magical paper.

2. Place the cup over the figurine. Then place the paper over the cup. Gently squeeze the paper until it forms around the cup.

3. Pick up the paper and cup to show that the figurine is still there. Hold the paper and cup slightly below the edge of the table and gently release the cup so it falls into your lap. The cup's form should remain in the paper.

4. Place the paper form over the figurine. With your other hand, smash the paper over the figurine.

5. Pick up the paper to reveal the figurine is still there. Tell your audience you accidentally made the cup disappear instead!

Disappearing Trick Tidbits

- In 1918, magician Harry Houdini appeared to make an elephant disappear before a live audience.

- One of magician David Copperfield's famous tricks involves making audience members disappear.

Magician Harry Houdini performs a trick.

- Many disappearing tricks done by professional magicians use mirrors to hide an object or person. But the mirrors must be perfectly clean. A streak or smudge will give away the trick!

Meet a Magician!

Criss Angel

Criss Angel is famous for doing magic tricks for people in public. Angel was born Christopher Nicholas Sarantakos in New York in 1967. He became interested in magic at age seven when his aunt taught him a card trick. As an adult, Angel performed tricks in public for his TV series, *Mindfreak*. In one episode, Angel makes a car disappear!

Glossary

gesture: a movement that helps express an idea or feeling

magician: a person who performs magic tricks

misdirection: the act of making someone pay attention to the wrong place

mystify: to confuse or puzzle

position: the way something looks or is placed in relation to what is around it

prop: an object a performer uses to create a certain effect

unique: unlike anything else that has been done

Further Reading

Funology — Disappearing Matchsticks
http://www.funology.com/disappearing
-matchstick/

Higginson, Sheila Sweeny. *Pulling Back the Curtain on Magic.* New York: Simon Spotlight, 2015.

Jay, Joshua. *Big Magic for Little Hands.* New York: Workman Pub., 2014.

Kelly, Kristen. *Abracadabra! Fun Magic Tricks for Kids.* New York: Sky Pony Press, 2016.

Kidspot — Amazing Disappearing Pencil Trick
http://www.kidspot.com.au/things-to-do/activity
-articles/amazing-disappearing-pencil-trick/news
-story/1a58ac5bf0a06cd6f1dc47a19f7eb83b?ref
=collection_view,magic-tricks

Magic Tricks for Kids — Disappearing Matchbox
http://magictricksforkids.org/disappearing
-matchbox/

Index

Photo Acknowledgments

The images in this book are used with the permission of: © Mighty Media, Inc., pp. 2, 6, 7 (top), 7 (bottom), 8, 9 (top), 9 (bottom), 10, 11, 12, 13 (top), 13 (middle), 13 (bottom), 14, 15 (top), 15 (bottom), 16, 17 (top), 17 (bottom), 18, 19; © iStockphoto, pp. 4, 5; © Shutterstock, pp. 20, 21.

Front cover: © Shutterstock.

Main body text set in Billy Infant.